D1505286

Published in 2017 by **Windmill Books**,
an Imprint of Rosen Publishing
29 East 21st Street, New York, NY 10010

Produced for Rosen by BlueAppleWorks Inc.
Creative Director: Melissa McClellan
Managing Editor for BlueAppleWorks: Melissa McClellan
Designer: T.J. Choleva
Editor: Kelly Spence
Puppet Artisans: Janet Kompare-Fritz (p. 10, 14, 16, 18); Sandor Monos (12 , 20); Jane Yates (22)

Picture credits: plasticine letters:Vitaly Korovin/Shutterstock; title page, TOC, Austen Photography; p. 4 Sony Pictures
Releasing/Photofest; p.5 Janet Kompare-Fritz; ; p. 6 left to right and top to bottom: ukrfidget/Shutterstock; Andrey Eremin/
Shutterstock; exopixel /Shutterstock; Lukas Gojda/Shutterstock; jocic/Shutterstock; koosen/Shutterstock; Irina Nartova/
Shutterstock; STILLFX/Shutterstock; Picsfive/Shutterstock; Darryl Brooks/Shutterstock; Winai Tepsuttinun/Shutterstock;
Yulia elf_inc Tropina/Shutterstock; Austen Photography; All For You /Shutterstock; Radu Bercan /Shutterstock; Austen
Photography; p. 7 left to right and top to bottom: Ilike/Shutterstock; Tarzhanova/Shutterstock; Austen Photography;
kamomeen /Shutterstock; Lesha/Shutterstock; ikurdyumov/Shutterstock; Austen Photography; Ilike/Shutterstock; p-8 to 27
Austen Photography; p. 28 left Valentina Razumova/Shutterstock; p. 29 upper left Warongdech/Shutterstock;p. 29 top right
Anneka/Shutterstock; p. 29 right taelove7/Shutterstock; p. 30, 31 Austen Photography

Cataloging-in-Publication Data
Names: Reid, Emily.
Title: Safari claymation / Emily Reid.
Description: New York : Windmill Books, 2017. | Series: Claymation sensation | Includes index.
Identifiers: ISBN 9781508192053 (pbk.) | ISBN 9781508192022 (library bound) | ISBN 9781508191964 (6 pack)
Subjects: LCSH: Animation (Cinematography)--Juvenile literature. | Sculpture--Technique--Juvenile literature. | Animals in art--
    Juvenile literature.
Classification: LCC TR897.5 R45 2017 | DDC 777'.7--dc23

Manufactured in the United States of America
CPSIA Compliance Information: Batch #BS16PK: For Further Information contact Rosen Publishing, New York, New York at 1-800-237-9932

Contents

What Is Claymation?

Get ready to take a walk on the wild side on a Claymation safari! Claymation, also known as clay **animation**, combines **stop-motion** animation with characters or puppets made out of modeling clay to create movies or short videos.

Stop-motion animation creates the illusion of movement when a series of still images, called **frames**, are quickly played in sequence. Each frame shows a slight change in position from the previous frame. Clay characters are easy to move and reposition to show these actions in small steps. The smaller the movements, the smoother the sequence appears. It takes several frames to make a Claymation movie. Animations can be created using many devices, including a traditional camera, smartphone, or tablet.

Full-length Claymation movies take months and lots of money to make. Often the latest technology is involved. In The Pirates! Band of Misfits, released in 3-D in 2012, some backgrounds were digitally created to show the rolling ocean waves.

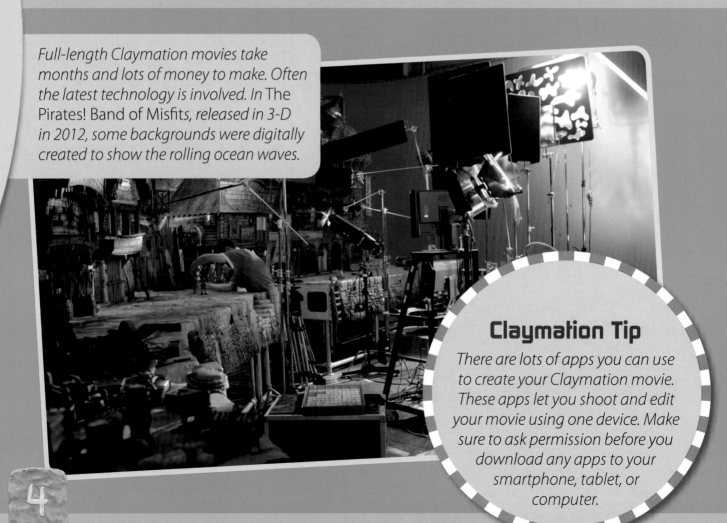

Claymation Tip

There are lots of apps you can use to create your Claymation movie. These apps let you shoot and edit your movie using one device. Make sure to ask permission before you download any apps to your smartphone, tablet, or computer.

All types of filmmaking, including Claymation, tell a story. To start, brainstorm an idea for your African safari. Think of a beginning, middle, and end. Write a short summary of the story. How many characters do you need to tell your story? What kind of background and props will you use?

When you make a Claymation movie, it is important to map out the character's movements before you start shooting. A **storyboard** is a series of drawings that show each step of the story. Use a storyboard to figure out what actions are needed, and in what order, to tell your story from start to finish. Sketch out each scene and label it with the scene number. After the storyboard is ready, it's time to create your puppets.

Scene 1

Scene 2

Scene 3

Scene 4

Scene 5

Scene 6

A storyboard showing six frames.

5

Materials and Techniques

Claymation puppets are created with nondrying, oil-based clay. Plasticine is a popular brand, although any nondrying modeling clay will do. This type of clay is moldable enough to create a character, flexible enough to allow that character to move in many ways, and dense enough to hold its shape when combined with a wire **armature**.

Materials That You Will Need

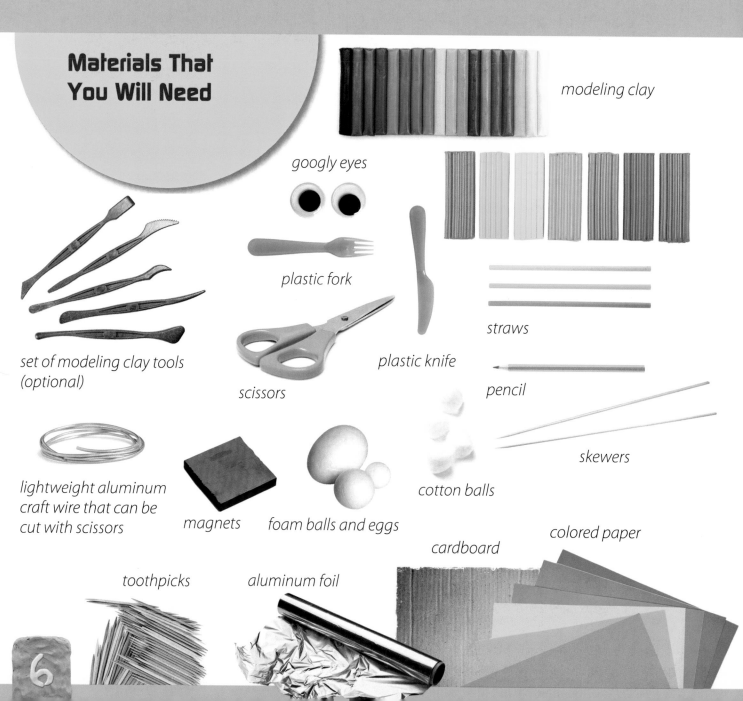

modeling clay

googly eyes

plastic fork

plastic knife

straws

scissors

pencil

set of modeling clay tools (optional)

skewers

lightweight aluminum craft wire that can be cut with scissors

magnets

foam balls and eggs

cotton balls

colored paper

cardboard

toothpicks

aluminum foil

Working with Clay

Modeling clay is oily and can be messy to work with. Prepare a work area. A piece of cardboard or foam board is great to work on. Wash your hands well when you finish working, as they will be oily, too.

Basic Shapes

All of these shapes can be made big or small or thin or thick, depending on the amount of clay used and the pressure applied. Use your fingers to squish, smooth, pinch, flatten, and poke the clay into whatever shape you want.

To form a ball, move your hands in a circle while pressing the clay lightly between them.

To create a pancake shape, roll a ball and flatten it between your thumb and fingers. Smooth the edges if they crack.

To make a snake shape, roll the clay on a flat surface with your fingers.

To form a teardrop, pinch and roll one end of a ball into a point.

To create a cylinder, roll a large piece of clay in your hand, then roll it on a flat surface to smooth. Press each end into the table to flatten it.

To make a slab, start with a large piece and flatten it on your work surface. Keep pressing the clay out and away from the center until it is as flat as you want it.

Modeling Tips

● Always start by kneading the clay in your hands to warm it up and soften it.

● You can mix different colors together to create new colors. Just squish the clay in your hands until it is blended completely or leave it partially blended to create a marble effect.

● Make your puppets about the same size as an action figure, between 4 and 6 inches (10 and 15 cm) tall. They should be big enough to move around but not so big they fall over.

Body Parts and Armatures

Puppets can be made in many ways. The simple ones require only modeling clay and some patience. If you decide to create more complicated puppets, you will need additional elements to give the puppets structure and support, such as wire armatures and foam shapes. It is a good idea to keep anything that is on top of the puppet light so it does not droop during animation. Using a lightweight foam ball should do the trick.

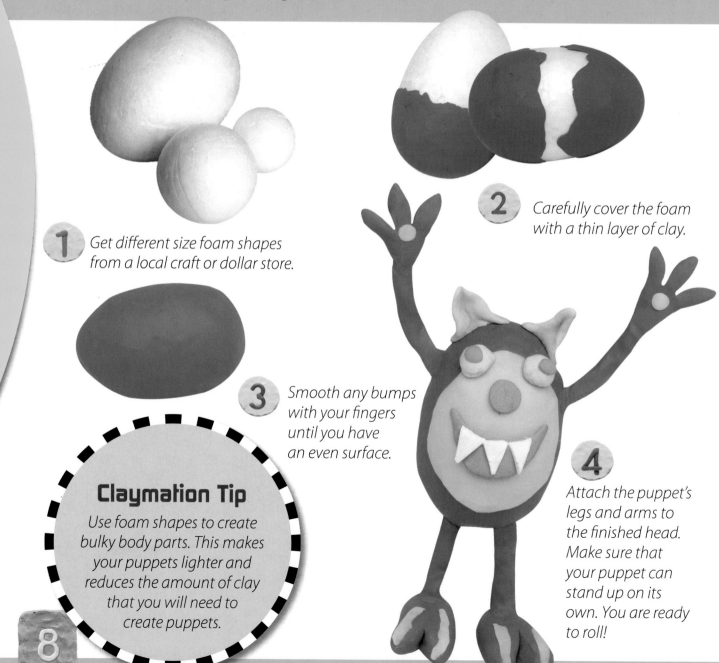

1 Get different size foam shapes from a local craft or dollar store.

2 Carefully cover the foam with a thin layer of clay.

3 Smooth any bumps with your fingers until you have an even surface.

4 Attach the puppet's legs and arms to the finished head. Make sure that your puppet can stand up on its own. You are ready to roll!

Claymation Tip

Use foam shapes to create bulky body parts. This makes your puppets lighter and reduces the amount of clay that you will need to create puppets.

Stability

Make sure your character has a big enough base or feet to support its weight. If necessary, you can stabilize it with putty or put pushpins through the puppet's feet to hold it in place.

Armatures

Armatures function as a skeleton that holds the puppet parts together and allows for them to move easily. Wire-based armatures are made using strands of lightweight wire. Whenever useful, you can combine an armature with foam pieces to create a base for your puppet. Make sure you don't make the clay too thick around the armature, or your puppet will be difficult to move.

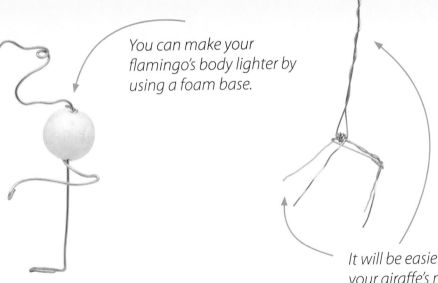

You can make your flamingo's body lighter by using a foam base.

It will be easier to animate your giraffe's movements if you use a wire-based armature for its neck and legs. Sometimes the shape of a puppet does not allow for the use of foam for its body.

Be creative with the details. Try new things. Use googly eyes on some puppets. Have fun with it!

An armature can be used for props as well. This tree would fall without its wire skeleton.

Crocodile Puppet

The Nile crocodile is the second largest reptile in the world. They live all over Africa near lakes, rivers, and marshlands. Nile crocodiles grow to an average length of 20 feet (6 m) and weigh a whopping 500 pounds (225 kg).

1 Use a lightweight foam ball for the body to make the puppet lighter. Roll a thin slab of dark green clay and cover most of the ball. Use a lighter green for the stomach. Add a little extra clay to the bottom.

2 Form the crocodile's legs out of two thick cylinders. Make the feet by rolling two oval balls and flattening them. Use a modeling tool to form toes. Push a toothpick through each leg to attach the feet as shown. Then attach the body.

3 Make two arms out of long cylinders. Pinch each arm until one end is narrower than the other. Form fingers at the narrow end. Attach the arms to the body using toothpicks.

4 Use two different colored cylinders for the crocodile's head. Flatten and join the two cylinders together at one end. Add an extra ball of clay to the end of the snout. Smooth the seams. Join the head to the body with a toothpick.

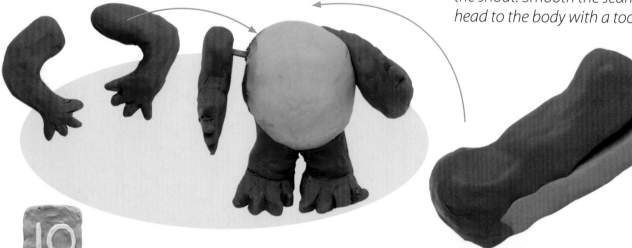

6

To make the eyes, roll two dark green ovals. Roll two smaller ovals in white, then two smaller ovals in black. Make two light green eyelids and assemble as shown. Press the eyes onto the crocodile's head.

5

Make the tail from a long, thin cylinder. Flatten it and mold one end to a point. Roll a long, light green snake. Gently flatten it, then pinch out a scalloped edge. Press the snake onto the tail, then press the tail onto the body.

7

Add sharp teeth and claws by pressing rice into the crocodile's mouth and hands. Use dark green clay to make eyebrows, a line down the snout, and spots on the feet. Decorate the body with ridges using a modeling tool.

Claymation Tip

When animating your crocodile, the toothpicks allow its body to move. You can turn the puppet's head from side to side and move its arms back and forth. If the crocodile has a lot to say, you can make it talk by gently moving the bottom of its snout up and down. Just make sure the teeth don't fall out!

Flamingo Puppet

The lesser flamingo lives in Africa. It is the smallest species of flamingo. These unique-looking birds have long, sticklike legs, curved necks, and pink feathers.

Use craft wire and a foam ball to make an armature as shown. Feed one long piece of wire through the center of the ball. Bend the wire into a neck and leg shape. Push a second piece of wire up through the ball. Loop the second wire firmly around the first. Then twist the second wire to form a bent leg. Hook the bottom of each wire to make the bird's feet.

Cover the entire armature in clay. Use different colors for the head, body, and legs.

3 Use a modeling tool to make the toes.

4 Make a flat pancake. Massage it into an oval shape and add a small triangle to the tip. Spread the pancake over the top of the bird's body and smooth the edges.

5 Press a googly eye into each side of the head.

6 Cover the beak with yellow clay. Add a small, curved clump of black to the end. Smooth the edges. Make a very thin black snake, then press and flatten it onto the side of the beak.

7 Roll four small snakes to make feathers for the top of the head. Group the snakes together and press them into the head. Curl the ends.

Claymation Tip

When animating your flamingo, have it perch near a clay lake or river. Gently press its foot into the table to make the flamingo stand.

Elephant Puppet

Elephants are the biggest animals that you will see on a safari. They are also the largest land animals in the world. Elephants use their flexible trunks to breathe, gather food, and suck up and spray water. A baby elephant, like the one shown here, grows long tusks before its first birthday.

1 For the legs, roll three cylinders using different colors of clay. One should be a bit bigger than the other two. Stack the cylinders on one another, with the larger one in the middle. Gently press down on the cylinders. Push a stick (or toothpick) through the middle of the stack. Repeat this step to make three more legs.

2 For the elephant's body, use your plastic knife to carefully remove the ends of a foam egg.

4 Cover the elephant's body, head, and trunk with a thin layer of clay. Add a bit of orange to the end of the trunk. Use your fingers to smooth the edges together. Add extra clay around the neck.

3 Insert two short pieces of craft wire into a small foam ball. This will be the elephant's head. Bend one wire into the shape of the elephant's trunk. Use the other piece to attach the head to the body.

5 Arrange the four legs under the body. Press the four sticks firmly into the foam.

6 For the eyes, roll two sets of blue balls, white balls, and black balls. Make two more tiny white balls as well. Flatten each ball slightly and press them together in this order: blue, white, black, and tiny white. Press the eyes into the head.

7 Make a large, flat teardrop shape for each ear. Use a different color to make a smaller teardrop, then press it into the larger one. Attach the ears to the head.

8 Make a small mouth and press it into the head, under the trunk.

9 Roll a small snake to form a tail. Press the tail into the backside of the elephant, then curl it. Roll several little balls. Flatten the balls onto the elephant's body for dots.

Claymation Tip

When animating your elephant, it can slowly shuffle across the savanna. Its trunk can swing from side to side or be used to pick up something, like a leafy, green snack.

Gorilla Puppet

You would be very lucky to see a gorilla on a safari. They are an endangered species. These highly intelligent primates live in the dense forests of Africa. Gorillas spend much of the day grazing. A male gorilla eats about 45 pounds (20 kg) of food each day.

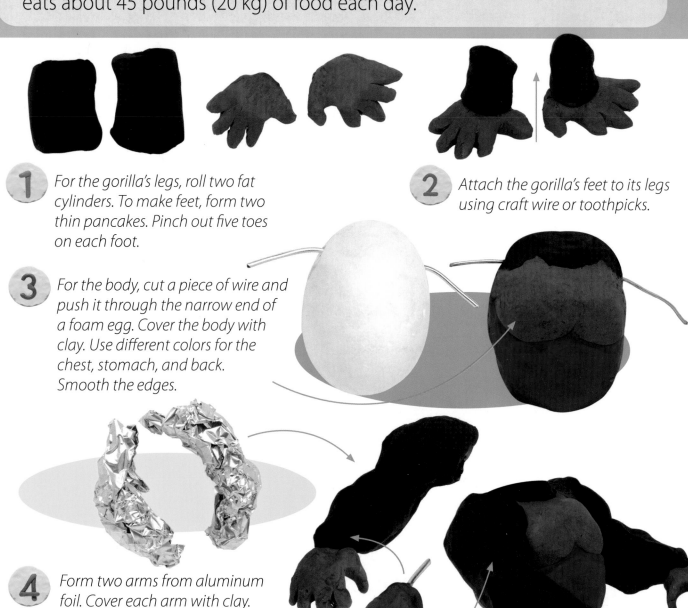

1. *For the gorilla's legs, roll two fat cylinders. To make feet, form two thin pancakes. Pinch out five toes on each foot.*

2. *Attach the gorilla's feet to its legs using craft wire or toothpicks.*

3. *For the body, cut a piece of wire and push it through the narrow end of a foam egg. Cover the body with clay. Use different colors for the chest, stomach, and back. Smooth the edges.*

4. *Form two arms from aluminum foil. Cover each arm with clay.*

5. *Make two hands using two small balls of clay. On each hand, pinch out five fingers. Use small pieces of wire to attach the hands to the arms. Then push the arms onto the wire armature to join them to the body.*

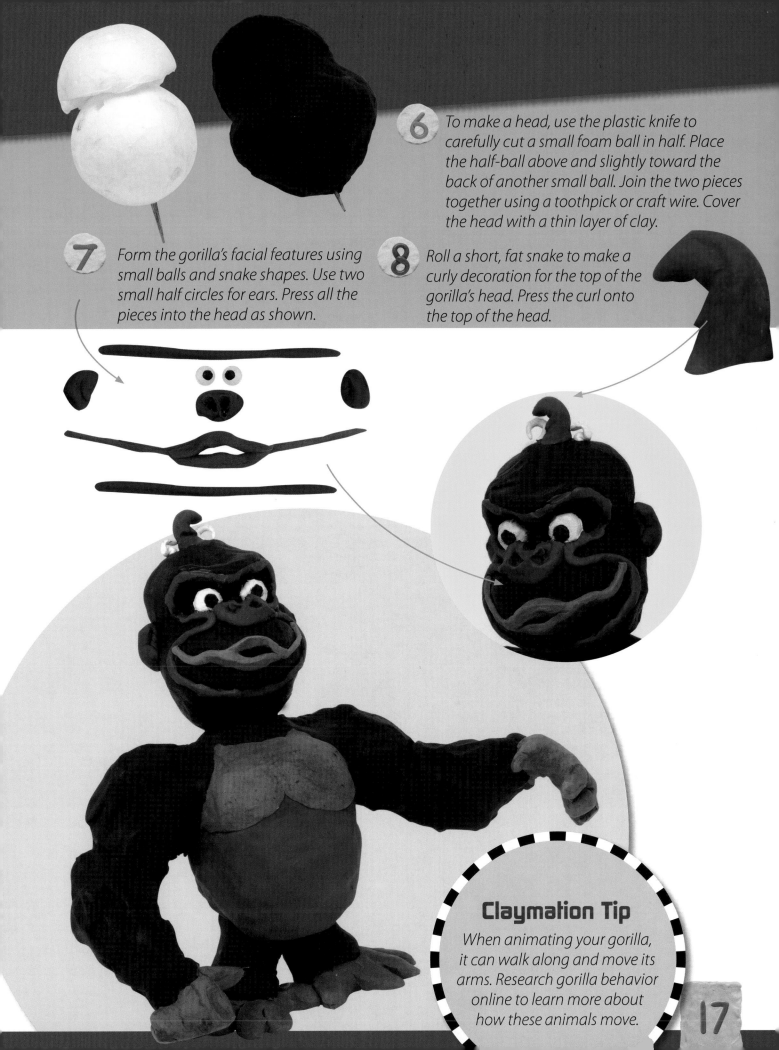

6 To make a head, use the plastic knife to carefully cut a small foam ball in half. Place the half-ball above and slightly toward the back of another small ball. Join the two pieces together using a toothpick or craft wire. Cover the head with a thin layer of clay.

7 Form the gorilla's facial features using small balls and snake shapes. Use two small half circles for ears. Press all the pieces into the head as shown.

8 Roll a short, fat snake to make a curly decoration for the top of the gorilla's head. Press the curl onto the top of the head.

Claymation Tip

When animating your gorilla, it can walk along and move its arms. Research gorilla behavior online to learn more about how these animals move.

17

Zebra Puppet

Zebras live on the African savanna. They are a member of the horse family and live in groups called herds. They have black bodies with white stripes and white bellies. Each zebra has a unique pattern of stripes.

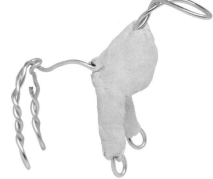

1 *To make this multicolored zebra, twist a long piece of wire into an armature as shown.*

2 *Soften a big ball of white clay. Start covering the armature. Use extra clay to form the zebra's broad chest.*

3 *Keep adding clay until the armature is covered. Leave the tips of the legs bare. Add additional clay to make the body and head fuller. Keep adding, pinching, and smoothing the clay until you are happy with the zebra's shape.*

4 *To make hooves, roll out four oval shapes. Press one hoof into each of the zebra's legs. Smooth the edges where the hooves meet the legs.*

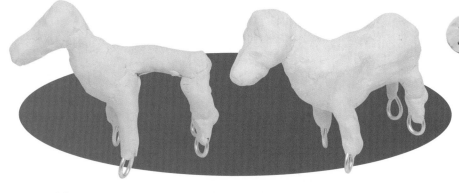

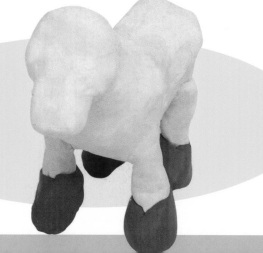

5 Roll several snake shapes using different colors of clay. (If you want to make a traditional zebra, use black.) Flatten the snakes, then press them into the zebra's head and body to form a striped pattern.

6 To make the eyes, use two small balls. Place a smaller blue ball on top of each. Press the eyes into the zebra's head. For ears, form two flat ovals. Pinch one end into a rounded point. Use a darker color for the inside of the ears. Add a thin strip of black to the top of each ear. Press the ears into the zebra's head.

7 Attach a square piece of clay to the end of the zebra's nose. Carve a mouth using the plastic knife. Smooth the edges.

8 Make a tail and mane using strands of string. Cut short pieces for the mane. Use longer pieces for the tail. You can use clay snakes to make the zebra's tail and mane, too.

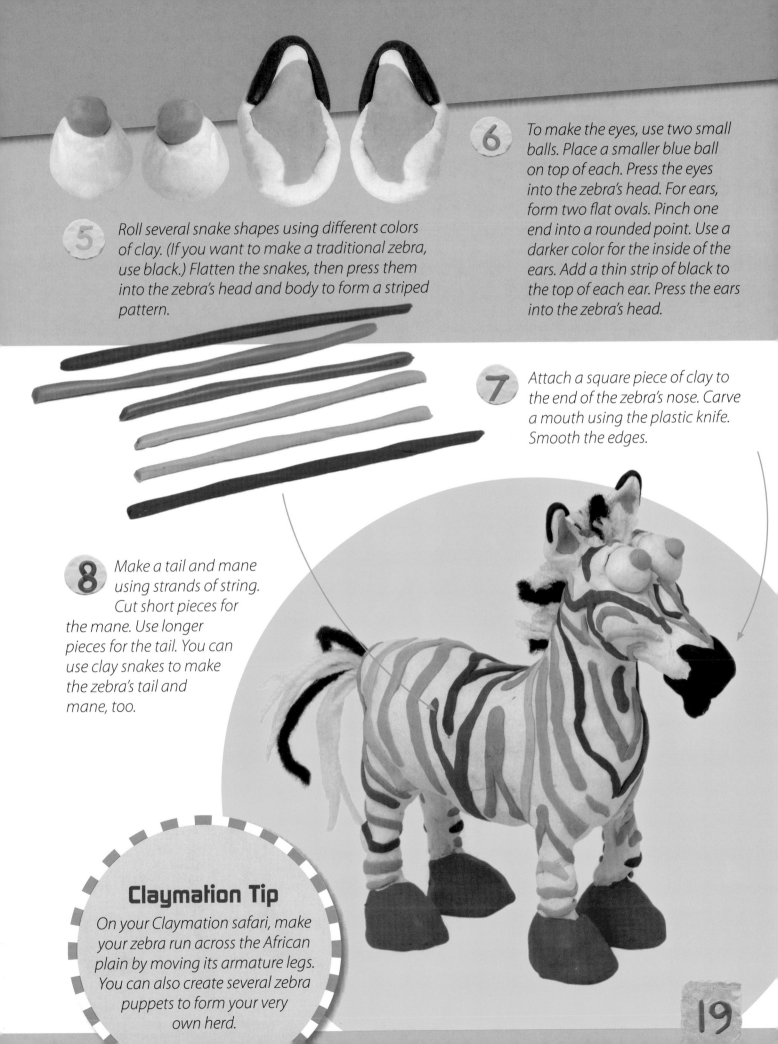

Claymation Tip

On your Claymation safari, make your zebra run across the African plain by moving its armature legs. You can also create several zebra puppets to form your very own herd.

Giraffe Puppet

The giraffe is the tallest land animal in the world. These towering animals stand between 14 and 19 feet (4 and 6 m) tall. They use their long necks to reach their favorite food, acacia leaves. Giraffes are a common sight on most African safaris.

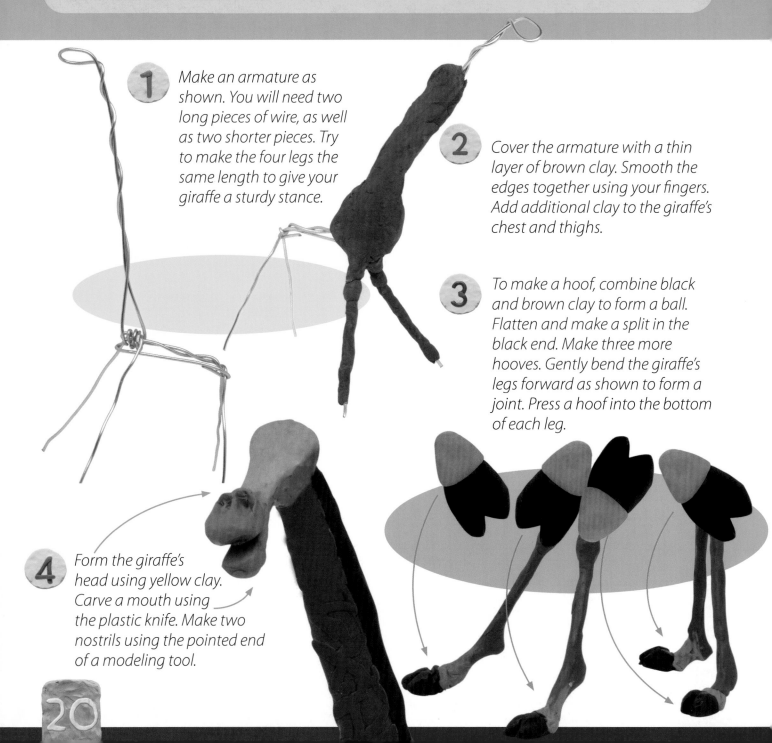

1 *Make an armature as shown. You will need two long pieces of wire, as well as two shorter pieces. Try to make the four legs the same length to give your giraffe a sturdy stance.*

2 *Cover the armature with a thin layer of brown clay. Smooth the edges together using your fingers. Add additional clay to the giraffe's chest and thighs.*

3 *To make a hoof, combine black and brown clay to form a ball. Flatten and make a split in the black end. Make three more hooves. Gently bend the giraffe's legs forward as shown to form a joint. Press a hoof into the bottom of each leg.*

4 *Form the giraffe's head using yellow clay. Carve a mouth using the plastic knife. Make two nostrils using the pointed end of a modeling tool.*

5 Make two flat oval shapes for the ears. Press each into the sides of the head. Roll two small black balls for eyes. Make an indentation in the face with a modeling tool. Press the two small balls into the indentations.

6 Use two small cylinders for horns. Press the horns into the top of the giraffe's head.

7 Roll a brown snake. Attach a black ball to the end. Press the tail into the backside of the giraffe.

8 Roll several yellow snake shapes. Flatten and press them onto the body creating a spotted pattern.

Claymation Tip

When animating your puppet, the giraffe can stroll across the set. Its long neck can be positioned to stretch high into a tree's branches or low to the ground.

Lion Puppet

The lion is the king of the savanna. Unlike most cats who live alone, lions live in groups called prides. A male lion has a thick mane of brown or black hair all around his head. Female lions, called lionesses, do most of the hunting for the pride.

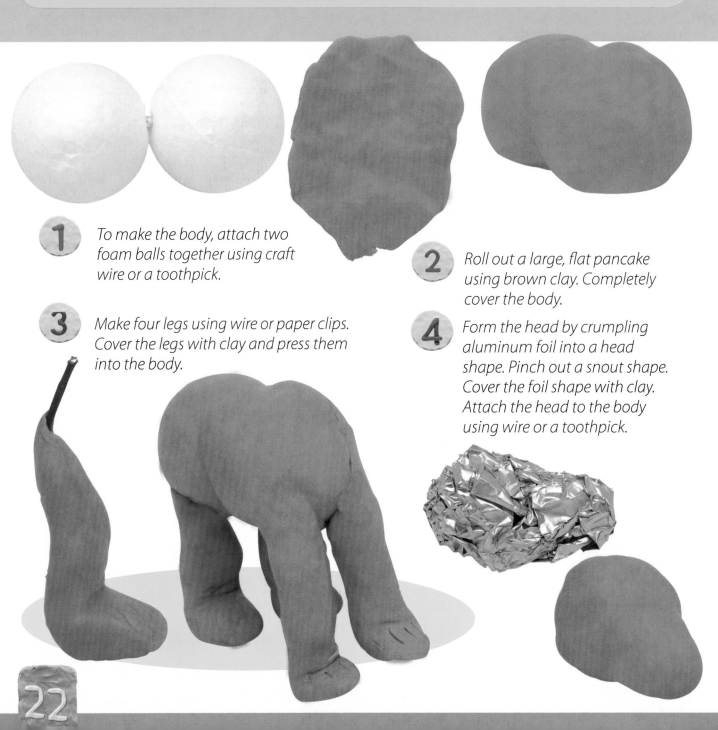

1 To make the body, attach two foam balls together using craft wire or a toothpick.

2 Roll out a large, flat pancake using brown clay. Completely cover the body.

3 Make four legs using wire or paper clips. Cover the legs with clay and press them into the body.

4 Form the head by crumpling aluminum foil into a head shape. Pinch out a snout shape. Cover the foil shape with clay. Attach the head to the body using wire or a toothpick.

5 Press out a white rectangle. Slice it into two pieces on a diagonal to make the lion's eyes. Add two black balls. Press the eyes into the head. Add eyebrows using thin black snakes. Make a nose out of a black triangle. Smooth white clay under the lion's chin.

7 Make the lion's mane by forming a large, flat pancake. Remove the center. Roll a long, yellow snake. Cut it into short pieces. Press the snakes onto the mane as shown.

6 Roll a brown snake shape. Attach a small black triangle to the tip. Fringe the triangle using a modeling tool. Attach the tail to the body.

8 Make ears by pinching two small pancakes into rounded triangles. Press the ears into the head.

Claymation Tip

In your movie, make the lion slowly stalk its prey across the savanna. To make a lioness, leave off the lion's mane.

The Props

Props are used in the creation of the movie. They decorate the set. Props add visual interest to the movie. Sometimes the puppets interact with them. Brainstorm ideas about what you might see on an African safari.

1 *Make acacia trees by creating a wire armature. Bend a piece of wire in half and cover it with clay. Add extra clay at the bottom to form a base. If you have moss, tear a piece off and attach it to the top of the tree. You can also make foliage out of a flat pancake of green clay. You can have a single tree or several standing together on your set.*

2 *Make grass using a lighter shade of moss. Form a flat oval, then press the moss into it. Make several patches. Arrange them on the set to create grasslands.*

3 *Make clay grass by mixing yellow and green clay together. Roll out a long, flat oval. Press it down at the bottom to create a base. Use scissors to cut fringe in the clay.*

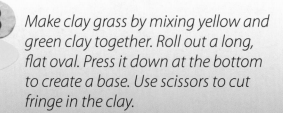

4 To make paper grass, fold a rectangular piece of green paper in half. Fringe one edge using scissors.

5 Make fluffy clouds using stuffing from an old stuffed animal or cotton balls. Cut a cloud shape out of white construction paper, then glue or tape the stuffing to the paper.

6 You can also make clouds out of clay. Make a thin white pancake. Pinch the edges into a scalloped shape. Make several clouds in different shapes and sizes.

7 Make a snake to hang from the acacia tree. Mix a few colors together, then roll out a snake shape. Add eyes and a mouth.

8 Make a river or lake by combining several shades of blue clay together. Squish and pinch your clay into a long, flat shape for a river or an oval for a lake.

Claymation Tip

Use two magnets to animate your clouds. Press one magnet into the back of the cloud. When you're ready to make your movie, put the cloud on the front of the set. Match the other magnet on the back. You can now make the cloud drift slowly across the sky in your film.

The Set

The set is where you will film your movie. It is the landscape in which your story will come to life. A set can be as simple as a piece of paper taped to the wall or more complex. The set needs to be large enough for your puppets to be able to move around.

Basic Set

The most basic set is a single piece of paper or poster board. Tape one end of the paper to the wall. Pull the paper and tape the other end to the table. Leave a bit of a curve in the paper.

1 You can build a simple set using a cardboard box. Break down the box and cut out two large rectangles that are the same size.

2 Line up the long sides of the rectangles and tape them together.

3 Make a triangle from the leftover cardboard.

4 Tape the triangle to the back of the one rectangle. Bend the other to form an L shape as shown.

5 Fold a piece of colored paper over the top of the box. Use clear or double-sided tape to secure each end of the paper to the front and back of the set.

6 Tear a piece of light colored paper to represent the dry African savanna. Line it up with the sides of the box and tape in place.

7 Arrange your props. Before you start shooting, secure the set to the surface you are working on with tape.

Try This!

Tear a piece of gray paper to make mountains looming in the distance. Glue or tape the paper to the set.

Tear a piece of green paper to make a faraway forest. Color along the bottom to indicate the dark undergrowth. Attach the trees to the set in front of the mountains.

Alternative Set

You can paint a background directly on the cardboard or paint a white piece of poster board and attach it to the cardboard.

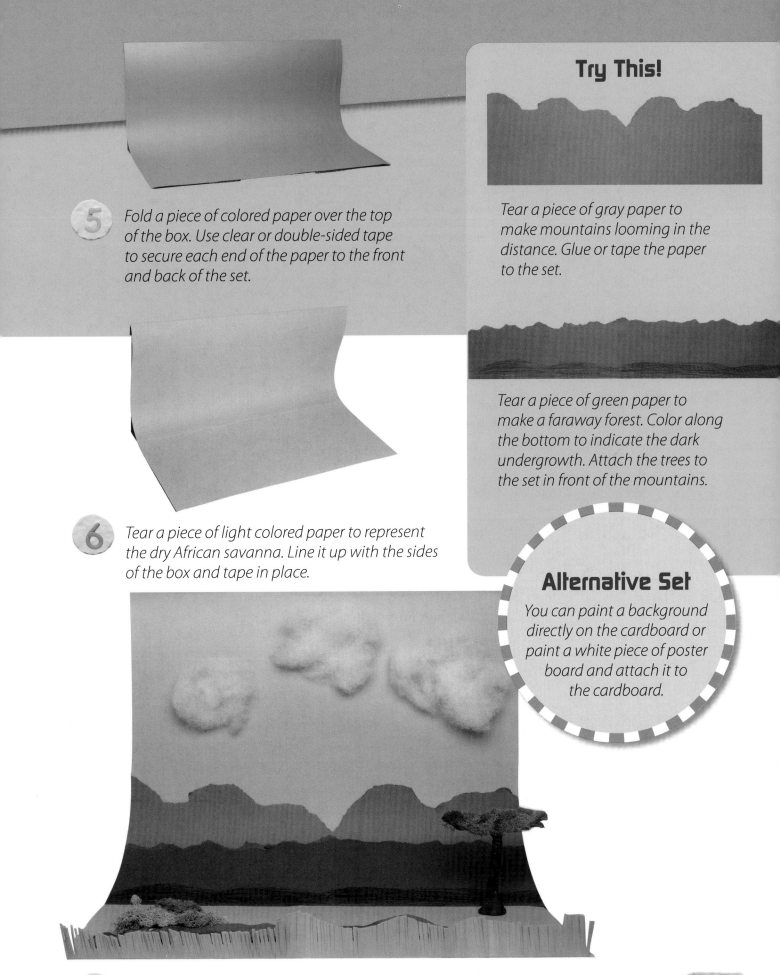

27

Lights, Camera, . . .

To light your set, a couple of desk lamps or the overhead lights should do the trick. Don't place your set near a window or shoot outside unless it is an overcast day. Changes in lighting will cause flickering in your movie.

Experiment with the placement of the lamps.
Take test shots to see how it looks.

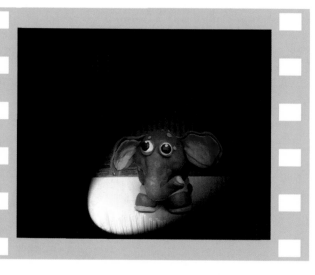

Flat, even light is created when two lamps are placed an equal distance apart. There are little or no shadows.

Place your elephant at center stage Create a spotlight by directing one light onto the set.

Claymation does not require a video camera. A digital camera, smartphone camera, or tablet camera will work. Think about the camera angles you want to use while shooting your film. The angle and distance from which you capture your scene can bring your movie to life.

In a straight-on shot, the camera is lined up directly with the puppet.

Shooting the movie from above makes the puppet appear small.

A closeup shot taken from a low angle can create a dramatic effect.

... Action! Making Your Movie

It's time to make your Claymation movie! You have your storyboard, your puppet(s), your set, lights, and camera. Position the puppets on the set when you are ready to begin. Using your storyboard as a guide, start taking photos. Make sure you move your puppets in very tiny increments. The smaller the movements, the smoother the film will be. Be careful not to move the camera while taking a sequence of shots.

You can use a camera on a tripod and import your stills later into an animation program. Or you can use your smartphone or tablet camera to capture photos directly in a stop-motion animation app.

Make sure your hands are out of the frame after moving the puppet before taking the next shot.

It takes a lot of patience to make a Claymation film. Slowly move your puppet toward an object on your set to make it appear as if the puppet is moving on its own. If the puppet moves too far in each shot it will appear to jump rather than move in one fluid motion.

Now it's time to finish your movie. **Postproduction** is the last step in creating your Claymation film. Within your app or animation program you can edit your frames, removing any that don't work. This is also the time to add music or sound effects. Music can set the mood of the film. Different types of music can sound happy, sad, or suspenseful. There are all kinds of free sound effects on the Internet, or you can record your own. Adding effects to your movie will bring the action to life.

Finally, it's showtime! Stage a screening to share your safari adventure with an audience. At the end, take a bow!

If there is a scene that doesn't work, cut it!

Use clay letters to make credits for your movie. Include a title and end credits, listing yourself and anyone else who helped.

GLOSSARY

animation In film, creating the illusion of movement using still images played in a rapid sequence.

armature A wire frame that acts as a skeleton for a sculpture made with modeling clay.

frame An individual picture in a series of images.

postproduction The final stages of finishing a movie after it has been recorded that usually involves editing and adding sound.

stop-motion An animation technique that uses a series of shots showing small movements to make characters or objects appear to move.

storyboard A series of pictures that show the scenes in an animation.

FOR MORE INFORMATION

FURTHER READING

Cassidy, John, and Nicholas Berger. *The Klutz Book of Animation.* Palo Alto, CA: Klutz, 2010.

Grabham, Tim. *Movie Maker: The Ultimate Guide to Making Films* Somerville, MA: Candlewick, 2010.

Piercy, Helen. *Animation Studio.* Somerville, MA: Candlewick, 2013.

WEBSITES

For web resources related to the subject of this book, go to: www.windmillbooks.com/weblinks and select this book's title.

INDEX